AF438455

God's Favorite Word, Come!

This is true whether God's speaks the word to us, or we speak the word to God. A familiar family prayer begins with the words, "Come Lord Jesus, be our guest…."

by

Rev. Kermit Rye

Copyright © 2021 Kermit Rye

ALL RIGHTS RESERVED

This work may not be used in any form,
or reproduced by any means,
in whole or part,
without written permission from the author.

ISBN: 9798732331097 (Paperback)

Cover photo by Kermit Rye
Book design by Kermit Rye

Printed by Kindle Direct Publishing
in the United States of America

to Doris
Steven
Michael
Sonja

In Appreciation

When you are called to serve a congregation, you immediately become part of a larger family of faith. You are welcomed into the homes of the congregation in times of happiness as well as in seasons of sorrow. It has been my privilege to serve the following congregations:

First Lutheran Church in Alexandria, MN (Internship 1956-57)

First Lutheran, Immanuel, and Our Savior's Wittenberg, WI (1958-61)

Immanuel and Brule Creek Lutheran, Elk Point, SD (1963-71)

American Lutheran, Grundy Center, IA (1971-86)

Estherville Lutheran, Estherville, IA (1986-96)

Grand Valley Lutheran, Rural Canton, SD (1996-99)

Visitation at East Side Lutheran, Sioux Falls, SD (2000-2021)

Table of Contents

God's Favorite Word 1

Happiness and Joy 2

Lost and Found 3

Christmas and Communication...4

Lord of Mountain and Valley 5

Tell us How to Die...6

Must Receive before Giving..7

Lord, Remember Me! 8

Top to Bottom 9

Going to the Father 10

Accounts of Christ's Resurrection..11

First Fruits of Harvest..12

Story with a Happy Ending..13

Special Kind of Servant 14

God's Presence Always 15

We Need to Forgive..16

Relationships Are Always Plural..17

The Good in Life Remembered 18

Swallow Up Death Forever..19

Trust Future to God..20

Jesus Is the Way..21

Paralyzed Man Walks...22

The Road of Service 23

Master of Wind and Wave...24

Nature of Temptation..25

On Being Found...26

Blood's Ability to Speak...27

Importance of Give in Forgiveness...28

The Aroma of Christ..29

Having Hope in God...30

Gratitude Brings Joy 31

Facing Life's Disappointments 32

God's Will vs Our Traditions 33

Experiencing Loss 34

Forgiving and Forgetting 35

Repentance a Change in Direction 36

Slow Down! Be Still! 37

God of Surprises 38

To Honor God's Name 39

A Person's Worth 40

Our Admission of Being Like Sheep 41

Jesus' Invitation to Come 42

Oldest Christian Hymn 43

Come, Thou Fount of Every Blessing 44

God's Favorite Word

A pastor whom I know spoke of God's "favorite word." God's favorite word, he said, is not the word "Forgiveness," or "Love." Not even the word, "Grace." But instead, God's favorite word is the word, "Come." When you begin to count how many times that word is used in the Bible it will surprise you.

Ho, everyone who thirsts," we read in Isaiah 55. "Come to the waters; and you who have no money, come, buy and eat. Come, buy wine and milk without money and without price." Then a bit further along, "Come to me; listen, so that you may live."

In John 6.35 Jesus is quoted as saying: "I am the bread of life. Whoever comes to me will never be hungry, and whoever believes in me will never be thirsty." Then in v.37: "Anyone who comes to me I will never drive away." In Matthew's Gospel (11.28) Jesus says: "Come to me all you who are weary and are carrying heavy burdens and I will give you rest."

A man named John Gough tells of sitting in church one Sunday. The congregation was singing the hymn, "Just as I am without one plea. He heard a hoarse, discordant voice behind him. The voice was so bad he couldn't help feeling sorry for its owner. Gough cringed as he listened to the grating voice without a hint of melody or awareness of what the tune should be. When the organist mercifully played an interlude, Gough felt a hand touch his arm and the man behind him whispered, "Could you tell me, please, the first words of the next verse? I believe I could pick up the rest if I knew how the verse begins."

John whispered back, "Just as I am, poor, wretched, blind...." As he turned to whisper the words, he looked into the face of the man with the awful voice and saw that the man was blind. Suddenly as he heard that grating voice trying to sing the next lines there was a beauty in the singing that had never come through before. "Sight, riches, healing of the mind—Yea, all I need in Thee to find. O Lamb of God, I come, I come."

The word "Come" is God's invitation to us. You who are discouraged even to the point of despair, God says, "Come. There is hope for you." You who need forgiveness, the way is now open. "Come." You who want to be assured of your salvation when this life ends, to you God says, "I have prepared the way for you myself. So, come!"

Happiness and Joy

The word "happiness" and the word "joy" are sometimes used interchangeably. They are similar, but certainly not the same. Between them there is a significant difference.

Picture with me an ocean. Wind and weather determine the conditions on the ocean's surface. In the absence of wind, the ocean is calm, but if violent winds are blowing, as with a hurricane, there are huge swells and steep waves. I once sailed out of New York harbor just ahead of a hurricane that struck the East Coast. The Queen Elizabeth I for those first two days was tossed about like a small toy in the water.

Happiness is like the ocean's surface. Our individual happiness is determined by "what is happening" in our lives. If our relationships are going well, if we are enjoying our work, and if we have our health, we probably have happiness too. But if any of the above cause trouble, we probably are not too happy. In fact, the word "happiness" comes from a three-letter Scandinavian word "hap" that means luck, or chance, or fortune. What has happened or is happening to us can determine how we feel.

Imagine with me this time the current deep within the ocean itself. That current flows steady and strong. It is unaffected by what is taking place on the surface. The current moves constantly, inexorably in one direction. It is the distant sun as it warms the water closer to the equator that causes those currents to flow. Only in recent times have we become more fully aware of the importance of those currents to the well-being of the planet itself.

Joy in a person's life is like those deep currents in the ocean. It is not determined by how things are going at any present moment, but on conditions that are deep within. For the Christian it is when God is satisfying the most important certainties of our existence. The Lord Jesus on the night before his death said to his followers: "I have said these things to you so that my joy may be in you, and that your joy may be complete."

Paul, in his letter to the Philippians writes, "Rejoice in the Lord always; again, I will say, rejoice." Throughout the letter he speaks of his own joy. For a man in prison, one would not expect Paul to be expressing this kind of joy. His inner attitude was not determined by outward circumstances. Paul was full of joy because he knew that whatever happened to him Jesus would be there for him. And if we place our trust and hope in Jesus, God's Son, he will be there for us as well!

Lost and Found

All of us know what it means to lose something valuable. We've had the frustration of wondering where it is. And then we have searched diligently to find it again. Luke in his Gospel tells how Jesus drew upon this common experience.

A group of very questionable people had come to hear Jesus. They were persons with bad reputations. The scribes and Pharisees were appalled. Didn't Jesus know what kind of people they were? So, they grumbled and said, "This man receives sinners and even eats with them!"

But Jesus came to their defense. He did so by telling three stories. In each one something gets lost—a sheep, a coin, and a boy. Then, what was lost is found. The shepherd brings home the sheep that strayed. The woman turns her house upside down to find the precious coin. At long last the Father welcomes home his wayward son. Each parable concludes with rejoicing. The entire village celebrates the return of the sheep that strayed. Having found her missing coin, the woman invites in the entire neighborhood. The Father throws the biggest party possible to celebrate his youngest son's return. "So, it is in heaven," Jesus said, "over one sinner who repents."

Let me share the story of a personal loss. I have a small appointment book that for me is irreplaceable. It preserves dates but also records other important information. I keep it in my shirt pocket during the day and on top of our dresser at night. One day, however, it was missing. I hunted for it everywhere. I tried to recall when I last used it.

Finally, I found it! It was in the closet in a different shirt I had worn a couple days before. I realized it had been there all the time and I breathed a sigh of relief. However, it gave me a new insight. All it takes for something to be lost is if it's not where it belongs!

Remember the older brother in Jesus' story. Something happened in his heart. He no longer shared his Father's concerns. He refused to look at things from his Father's point of view. He never left home, but he ended up more lost that his younger brother ever was. In that home there was a younger son who *STRAYED* and an older brother who *STAYED*. Both, however, needed to repent.

Two questions come to mind. As a result of our Lord's stories, did any of his critics that day ever have a change of heart concerning those who came to hear him? More importantly, will there be any rejoicing in heaven because you and I have repented of OUR sins?

Christmas and Communication

Each year in the weeks before Christmas, my wife and I send a letter to people that we know. This includes family members, close friends, as well as members of congregations we have served. When you send a sizeable number of letters, you tend to get a lot of mail in return.

Some years ago, as my wife and I were preparing our annual Christmas letter, we were also addressing over a hundred envelopes in which to send them. My wife made an interesting comment: "Everything could be taken away from Christmas—the gifts, the special baking, the decorations, the tree—everything but the cards and letters. They are what makes Christmas special." Then she added: "Christmas is communication!"

There is a passage from the New Testament that says, "Long ago, God spoke to our ancestors in many and various ways by the prophets. But in these last days God has spoken to us by a Son…He is the reflection of God's glory and the exact imprint of God's very being…." In other words, God's clearest message came to us when he sent Jesus to this world. If someone were to ask, "What is God like?" A good answer would be, "Look at Jesus. He is God's Son!"

Have you ever wondered why it is we make a special effort to communicate with others at Christmas? We do this more than any other time during the year. God sent the first Christmas message about the birth of His Son. It was delivered by a host of angels to some lowly shepherds within walking distance of the event itself. Maybe that is why we make the effort to get in touch during this special season

Lord of Mountain and Valley

Our Lord led his followers to a secluded area in the northern part of Palestine. It was there he asked the disciples who they thought he was. Peter spoke for himself and the others when he said that Jesus was the Messiah. Then, for the first time, our Lord shared what being the Messiah involved.

A short time later, Jesus singled out three of his disciples and took them with him up a high mountain. While there, he was transfigured before them. His face shone like the sun and his clothes became dazzling white. Two from Old Testament times appeared and talked to Jesus—Moses who had been with God on Mt. Sinai and Elijah who had encountered God at Mt. Horeb. To prolong the vision, Peter suggested they build three shelters--one for Jesus, one for Moses, and one for Elijah.

It was then a cloud moved in and obscured the disciple's vision. They heard a voice out of the cloud saying: "This is my own dear Son. Listen to him!" When the disciples finally opened their eyes, all they saw was Jesus. As they retraced their steps back down the mountain, Jesus told them not to tell anyone about the experience until he had been raised from the dead!

Based on this account of the Transfiguration, we might be tempted to ask: "What should we be promoting today--visions from God like those the disciples experienced? Spiritual ecstasies or voices from the heavens? There may be a hunger for this type of experiences.

I think of a career military officer, seldom home and even less in church. Then, one day, he and his small son were in a car accident. For days the boy hovered between life and death. The man's prayers and those of others were offered. Through the miraculous recovery of his son, this father saw a new light. The continuing glory was still visible as he shared the experience with me following worship one Sunday morning when he and his young family were visiting his parents.

It is true that some may have spiritual comets streak through their lives. But if we are not one of those who do, let's remember—only three of the disciples got to experience this vision. When you measure this against the twelve, that's a rather small percentage. We may have to rely on the testimony of others that Jesus is indeed, "Lord of the Mountain." But there is that word of promise, that Jesus is even more so, "Lord of the Valley!" And it is in the valley that most of us will live out our lives.

Tell us How to Die

It happened in England during the 2ndWorld War. One night there was a huge party put on by the USO. Hundreds of American soldiers attended. All of them were expecting to take part in the invasion of the mainland of Europe. We know now that over 125,000 American soldiers lost their lives in that invasion. Everyone present that evening was aware that what was called "D-Day" could be soon

At the end of the activities, a young sergeant was asked to offer a word of thanks for the group. He did so by saying how much they had all enjoyed themselves. But then he showed what was on everyone's mind. In his concluding remarks he blurted out, "Now is there anyone here who can tell us how to die?" No one present volunteered.

However, I believe Jesus is one who can answer that question. He did so for a group of his own disciples. His words are recorded in the 14th chapter of John's Gospel. Speaking to this bewildered group of men who were sensing death was just around the corner, Jesus said, "Let not your hearts be troubled. Believe in God, believe also in me. In my Father's house are many rooms. If it were not so, would I have told you that I go to prepare a place for you? And when I go and prepare a place for you, I will come again and will take you to myself, that where I am, there you may be also."

Then Jesus added, "And you know the way where I am going." Thomas, always the one to ask questions, said, "Lord, we do not know where you are going; how can we know the way?" Jesus said to him, "I am the way…No one comes to the Father but by me!"

When I go on a journey, I want the use of a reliable map, or at least accurate directions from someone who has made the trip before. It is exasperating to lose my way and not make it to where I want to go. What more important journey is there than the one we take at the end of life when we leave this world and travel into eternity? The Bible tells us that our Lord made that journey for each of us. He did so when he died upon the cross. As our turn comes to experience death, Jesus is prepared to show us the way as well. I am convinced that, if we place our trust in him, he will bring us safely to our destination.

Must Receive before Giving

Flight attendants give instructions to passengers who have boarded an airplane that is readying for takeoff. Parents of children receive special guidance. They are told that if oxygen masks drop down from storage compartment above, they are to put the mask on themselves before they assist any child seated beside them.

This may sound counter intuitive. Shouldn't they help a child with their mask first? But when you think about it, it does make sense. A person can't help another if they have become incapacitated themselves. You should take care of your own need for oxygen before you can assist someone else needing to do the same.

We are reminded of what happened that night in the upper room. It was the evening before Jesus was soon to give up his life upon the cross. During the meal, our Lord wrapped a towel around his waist and assumed the role of a servant. He began washing his disciples' feet. When he came to Peter, the impetuous disciple refused: "You shall never wash my feet," Peter said. But the Lord issued a warning. "Unless you let me wash you, you have no share with me."

Jesus appears to be telling him, "Unless you are willing to receive, you have nothing to give?" Remember the time you agreed to teach a Sunday school class, and then one day realized that you had become the main student in the class! All too quickly we discover that we have nothing to give until we first receive.

In the same way there needs to be receptivity on our part if we expect to be of service to others. The Apostle Paul in one of his letters asks these questions, "What do you have that you did not receive? And if you received it, why do you boast as if you had not received it?" It would be wise to remember that all of us are dependent upon the One from whom all good gifts come.

Lord, Remember Me!

Three crosses were on that hill and three men were about to die. Two were criminals; one on the right, the other on the left, and Jesus in the middle. A conversation was taking place between the two convicts. In anger and pain, the first had lashed out at Jesus: "If you are the Messiah, get us down from here," he had cried. "Save yourself and us!" It was more a command than a request.

But the other criminal scolded him. "Since you are soon to meet God," he said, "shouldn't you show a little respect? We have been condemned to die and we had it coming. But this man has done nothing wrong." And then, looking up into the face of Christ, the second criminal made one last request: "Jesus," he pleaded, "remember me when you come into your kingdom."

From where did such faith come? How could one so tangled and torn by life have thought to make such a request and at the last moment possible? Faith, we understand, is God's gift too. It is not just the salvation that becomes ours through faith, but the ability to believe, the capacity to trust. And this man had somehow received that gift even as life was slipping away.

"Lord, remember me…." he pleaded. It was such a simple request. But it was spoken urgently and with confidence in the One to whom it was addressed. And from Jesus there was that immediate reply: "Truly I tell you, today—this very day—you will be with me in Paradise!" In one moment, a man not fit to live on earth with other human beings was in the next moment fit to live in Heaven with God. Such is the incredible miracle of God's mercy, and the transforming power of God's grace.

A verse in the New Testament says: "For while we were still weak, at the right time Christ died for the ungodly. Indeed, rarely will anyone die for a righteous person— though perhaps for a good person someone might dare to die. But God proves his love for us, in that while we were yet sinners Christ died for us." (Rom.5.6-8)

Top to Bottom

The agony Jesus would have experienced on the cross is impossible for us to imagine. He had been suspended there for several hours held only by nails driven through his hands and feet. The Gospel of Mark tells us that at 3:00 o'clock in the afternoon, "Jesus gave a loud cry and breathed his last. And the curtain of the temple was torn in two, from top to bottom."

The curtain to which Mark refers was an elaborate one that hung in the temple in Jerusalem. Its purpose was to cover the opening to an inner room called the Holy of Holies. Jews believed it was in that room God chose to dwell. The curtain demonstrated the separation that existed between God and humanity. It served to keep God in and to keep people out. No one was allowed to enter this sacred place except the High Priest, and he could do so only once a year. On "the Day of Atonement," he would bring with him the blood of animals sacrificed for his sins and the sins of the people. He would sprinkle this blood upon the sacred articles kept there.

Mark says it was at the very moment Jesus died outside the city that, "the curtain of the Temple was torn in two from top to bottom." Notice! It does not say bottom to top. Salvation begins, not with us, but it begins with God. It is because of what God accomplished through Jesus' death and resurrection that we now have access to God's presence.

The sinfulness of humanity always stood in the way of God being able to accept us. And just knowing how life was to be lived was never enough. It took the coming of Jesus to live life as God wanted it lived. Then, this sinless Son of God willingly took upon himself our sins and the sins of all humanity. For those sins he suffered and died upon that cross. However, on the third day God raised him again from the dead.

Death was to be the punishment for sin. Jesus accepted the punishment we deserved, and in doing so made it possible our receiving the gift of eternal life. The Bible says: "God made him to be sin for us, who knew no sin, that we might become the righteousness of God in him." In the New Testament Letter to the Romans we have this additional promise: "There is therefore now no condemnation for those who are in Christ Jesus."

Going to the Father

I was surprised recently to discover that Jesus said the exact same thing five times to his disciples the night before his crucifixion. To quote only three of them: (John 14.12) "The one who believes in me…will do greater works than these, because "I am going to the Father." (John 14.28) "If you loved me, you would rejoice that I am going to the Father." (Jn.16.28) "I am leaving the world and am going to the Father."

A pastor was walking down the airport ramp to board a plane. A family of four was just ahead of him. The mother was carrying the youngest child and the father was holding their little girl by the hand. She appeared to be about four and obviously was excited and looking forward to the trip. Her father looked down at her and asked, "Where are we going?" "To Grandma's!" she shouted. The pastor observed that she didn't say, "To Bismarck or to Billings," but "to Grandma's." As far as she was concerned, she was going to a person, the place was secondary.

One of the best stories I know involved a patient and his doctor. A man was told he was terminally ill with cancer. It was just a matter of time that he could live. His one wish was that he could spend his final days at home. Several family members were determined he should have his wish fulfilled, and the man's physician was willing to make "house-calls" that were essential.

One day when the Doctor came to see him, they were both in the upstairs bedroom where the man now lived. The doctor was going about his work in caring for his patient. The man knew his physician was a Christian and so he asked him, "What do you think Heaven is like?" The Doctor didn't stop what he was doing. He kept right on with his work. Several minutes went by and the man wondered if he would even get an answer.

Finally, the doctor paused and repeated the question: "You asked me what I think Heaven is like. When I came to your house today, I brought my dog along. In fact, he's right outside the front door. He doesn't know anything about this house—the fact it's a two-story home, or that you are here in this upstairs bedroom. He doesn't know anything about this house except one thing. He knows I'm here, and he wants to get in. To me," he said," that's what Heaven is like."

Jesus did not say, "I'm returning to the place from which I came," or, "I'm on my way back to Heaven." He said, instead, "I am going to the Father." We need to realize that when we leave this life our primary destination is to be with the Father!

Accounts of Christ's Resurrection

I was meeting with a new-member class in a former parish that I served. In one of the sessions we examined the Gospels accounts of Jesus' resurrection. Each account tells how devoted women went to the tomb early that Sunday morning expecting to find their Lord's body. Instead, they met an angel or angels who told them that Jesus had been raised from death. He was now alive, and they were to go and inform his disciples.

I pointed out that even though each of the accounts reports the central fact of Jesus being raised from the dead, there are several other details that are different. Matthew names two women who went to the tomb, while Mark says there were three. Luke says there were more than three and John speaks of only Mary Magdalene. Matthew and Mark report the appearance of one angel while Luke and John say there were two. Matthew and Luke say the women gave the message of the resurrection to the disciples, but Mark describes how the women "fled from the tomb terrified and said nothing to anyone." John says that when Mary brought the incomplete news of the tomb being empty, Peter and the "other disciple" went to investigate.

It was at this point that a member of the class shared an important insight. He worked in the insurance industry and it was his responsibility to meet with those who had experienced any kind of loss. The illustration he shared was about a family whose barn had burned. Some days after the fire, he met with the farmer, his wife, and two of their children. Their discussion was held around the kitchen table.

But, as the family began describing the sequence of events leading up to and including the fire, each of the family members had a different version. They began arguing among themselves and took issue with each other's story. The only thing for certain was that the barn had burned to the ground. The person who shared this said that their disagreement was the clearest evidence to him that the fire had not been set by anyone in the family. Otherwise they would have had a more unified account.

If the early Church had come up with a fabricated story of Christ's resurrection, they would have made the effort to get their accounts to agree. But because they dealt with something that happened there are different versions from those involved in the events themselves. In the surprise and excitement of Christ's resurrection, is it any wonder there are differences in several of the less important details?

First Fruits of Harvest

As a boy, I remember going with my father into the cornfield. It happened in the fall of the year. I watched him check to see how well the ears of corn had filled out. Most of the checking he did by feeling several ears still inside the husk. But once in awhile he would pull back the husk to make a visual inspection.

However, before we left the field that day, he would select one ear of corn. It was the largest and best he could find. He snapped it from the stalk where it had grown. As we headed back to the house, he would tie the husk into a knot.

In the entryway of our home there was a pair of bullhorns attached to the wall. They normally served as a hat rack. But it was there he would hang that ear of corn. It was the first one he harvested that year. In looking back, I realize that for him it must have been a sign of hope. If he could find an ear of corn like that in the field, then we could be assured of a harvest. There was more to come.

There is something like that in Scripture in the 15th chapter of 1st Corinthians. To a group of people who were beginning to doubt there would be a resurrection, Paul wrote: "But in fact Christ has been raised from the dead. He is the first fruit of those who have died." (v.20)

It is because God raised Jesus from the dead, we can be assured God will raise us to life again as well. In the African American spiritual, "My Lord, what a Morning," there is a haunting refrain, "to wake the nations underground..." It is in response to a trumpet sound, a cry, and a shout. Jesus is indeed the first fruits of all who sleep the sleep of death. There is a day of harvest coming when God will wake the dead, so death will not be the final answer.

Story with a Happy Ending

A little boy was promised he could have a puppy for his birthday. When his father took him to the pet shop, there was a whole menagerie of dogs from which to choose. He stood there trying to make up his mind. Finally, his father said, "Which one do you want? You're going to have to decide!" Pointing to one of the puppies furiously wagging its tail the little boy said, "I'll take the one with the happy ending."

All of us like a story with a happy ending. But no story is quite like the story of Easter and of Jesus' resurrection. One of the resurrection appearances of our Lord tells how the disciples were huddled together behind locked doors. They had gathered there out of fear. The account goes on to say, "Jesus came and stood among them and said, 'Peace be with you."

It was the darkest time in the life of the Lord's followers. For good reason they were behind locked doors. If Jesus had been killed, what hope was there for them? But God had planned a surprise! Suddenly Jesus appeared and stood among them and said, "Peace be with you."

Some of us may be living behind locked doors too. A tragedy of one form or another has engulfed our life. It could be that a relationship has been broken—a new wound exposed. There is a feeling of emptiness that just can't be filled. It might be a financial crisis and there are clouds of uncertainty ahead. It might be an illness in our life or the life of someone we love. We have withdrawn behind four walls and now live in fear of the future. Before we had freedom to come and go as we pleased, but now there is a kind of imprisonment. Doors for us are closed and barred.

It is to us Christ appears and speaks those words, "Peace be with you." You don't have to face these problems alone, for I am with you. In effect he is saying, My Father's raising me to life again makes all the difference in the world for you and for all who believe in me. There is hope for your future. A postscript to this passage says, "Now Jesus did many other signs in the presence of his disciples which are not written in this book. But these are written so that you may come to believe that Jesus is the Messiah, the Son of God, and that through believing you may have life in his name."

Special Kind of Servant

"Here is my servant whom I uphold, my chosen in whom my soul delights...." With these words Isaiah begins the first of what are called, "Servant Songs." The Prophet then describes what kind of person this future servant will be. "A bruised reed he will not break and a dimly burning wick he will not quench."

In this short description we have two pictures. The first is of someone making a flute out of a reed. The flute-maker discovers a flaw in the reed he has been carving. What should he do? Reeds grew by the thousands down along the Jordan. Obviously, he could break the damaged reed in two and choose another from the seemingly endless supply. But No, the Prophet says. The flute-maker doesn't do that. Instead, he works patiently with that bruised reed until it became the instrument, he first envisioned it to be.

The second picture is of a woman preparing a lamp as evening comes. Her lamp is a rather simple device, shaped like a saucer with a handle at one end and a lip at the other. The saucer is filled with oil and a twisted rag serves as the wick. The end that extends beyond the lip is lighted. Hopefully the lamp will give light to her darkened room. But not tonight! The flame sputters and spews smoke instead. What should she do? Simplest would be to take that worthless rag and throw it away. She could easily choose another piece of cloth and start all over again. But she doesn't. The housekeeper refuses to give up on that old rag. She painstakingly trims and shapes it until it provides light for her darkness. The Servant whom God sends will treat people the same way, the prophet says.

Many centuries later, when the New Testament was being written, the gospel writers delighted in showing how Jesus fulfilled Old Testament prophecies. This was especially true for Matthew. In a chapter where he tells how Jesus showed compassion by healing a man with a withered hand, he then inserts this prophecy from Isaiah. Matthew attributed Isaiah's description of this persistent flute-maker and the patient housekeeper to Jesus. "A bruised reed he will not break and a dimly burning wick he will not quench." It was as if to say, this is the way the Lord treats those with imperfect lives.

It was true then and is true today. No matter what problems we have, or what shortcomings are ours, God could easily give up on us. But the Lord doesn't! We, whose lives are flawed and whose failings are so obvious, could justifiably be cast aside. Instead the Lord demonstrates patience and persistence as he continues working with us.

God's Presence Always

There was a two-person drama used on the Chautauqua circuit years ago that always brought a response from the audience. On center stage was a solitary streetlight. A man would appear obviously looking for something. Finally, he was on his hands and knees beneath the streetlight still searching.

Moments later a policeman would saunter on stage twirling his nightstick. Noticing the man beneath the streetlight he would approach and ask, "Did you lose something?" "Yes," the man replied, "my keys." So, the policeman would join in his search.

Finally, the policeman would ask, "Are you sure you lost them here?" The man on the ground would answer, "No, I think I lost them over there," pointing offstage. "Well then, why are you looking for them here?" the policeman asked. "Because the light is here!" the man replied.

There is something similar that happens in our lives too. We make the mistake of thinking God can be present only when things are going well for us. God can only be near when all is sweetness and light. Then, when darkness settles in, we think God has abandoned us. How can God be present when we are experiencing pain and trouble?

Yet, for the person of faith, that can be when God is nearest of all. Listen to the word of the Lord spoken through the Prophet Isaiah to ancient Israel (43.2-3): "When you pass through the waters, I will be with you, and through the rivers, they shall not overwhelm you. When you walk through fire you shall not be burned and the flame shall not consume you; for I am the Lord your God, the Holy One of Israel, your Savior."

In New Testament times when life was difficult for the Apostle Paul, God spoke words of reassurance to him (2 Cor. 12.9). Paul had prayed several times that a troublesome problem in his life would be removed, but the problem remained. Finally, the Lord said to me, 'My grace is sufficient for you (Paul), for my strength is made perfect in weakness.' So," he concludes, "I will all the more gladly boast of my weaknesses, that the power of Christ may rest upon me." The Lord's promise that each of us can claim is where he says (Heb.13.5), "I will never leave you nor forsake you."

We Need to Forgive

"Forgive us our trespasses as we forgive those who trespass against us." In teaching his disciples how to pray, Jesus linked these two together. As we ask God to forgive us, we then affirm our willingness to forgive others. The Lord has written something into the very fabric of life. If we refuse to forgive someone, we somehow make it impossible to experience God's forgiveness.

Some years ago, I experienced a very hurtful situation. A man accosted me one Monday morning, accusing me of writing an article that had appeared in the local paper the previous week. The article had questioned this man's judgment in arranging an athletic banquet on what the community recognized as "church night." I happened to be out of town that weekend, so he had several days to build up steam.

This man's tirade occurred in a very public place. He used abusive language, some of which I had heard used before and some of which I hadn't. At first, he gave no opportunity for me to set the record straight. To put it mildly, he was livid.

When he finally gave me a chance to speak, I clarified that I had not written the article. Another pastor in the community had composed it. I did explain that it expressed the sentiments of many of the pastors, since confirmation classes, choir rehearsals, etc. in each of the parishes had been affected. As the conversation wound down, he apologized, and I accepted his apology. However, I soon realized I had only spoken the words. Deep down, I had not forgiven him! C.S. Lewis is quoted as saying, "Forgiveness is a great idea, until you have something to forgive!"

I soon realized my attitude towards this man was hindering my own relationship with God. My prayers didn't seem to get any further than the ceiling. I tried to figure out what was wrong. Then I remembered Jesus' command, "Love your enemies, do good to those who hate you, bless those who curse you, pray for those who abuse you."

I began trying to do that. I prayed daily that God would bless this man in his work, in his family, in all aspects of his life. I prayed more for this man in those next few months than I did for anyone in the parish I was serving. About two years later he was the MC for a community event in which I had a part. As he introduced me that day, I realized his attitude towards me had changed. I knew my attitude towards him had changed completely long before.

Forgiveness has a way of setting us free.

Relationships Are Always Plural

"I was ready to be sought out by those who did not ask, to be found by those who did not seek me. I said, 'Here I am, here I am.' to a nation that did not call on my name." God was describing a deep desire to be in relationship with the nation of Israel. This longing was expressed through the words of the prophet Isaiah.

I know I am stating the obvious when I say that, "It takes two to have a relationship." From the Isaiah passage quoted above, we learn that even God is faced with this limitation. Apparently, God can't have a relationship with the people of a nation, or with an individual, if they are not open to that relationship! I once heard a pastor say that, "God loved the world so much that God even created a place for those who did not want anything to do with Him." The pastor then went on to say, "That place is Hell."

We read in the Book of Acts that, "God is not far from every one of us." That would include you and me--but also the agnostic and the atheist. This New Testament passage seems to suggest that life on this earth is livable because God is still present in our world. If it is true, that Hell is the place God provides for those who want nothing to do with him, try to imagine what it will be like for them in eternity if God were totally absent!

I know that Scripture gives glimpses of what Hell is like. The Book of Revelation refers to Hell as "the lake of fire." And Jesus once told a story about two drastically different conditions of existence after death. He first told about a man named Lazarus who, when he died, found himself in the embrace of Abraham, the man of faith. Jesus went on to also tell about a well-to-do man who in the hereafter was desperately thirsty. His deepest regret was that, in his life on earth, he had left no room for God. His material wealth had been given priority.

This second man was informed it was too late for him to have a change of heart. He then requested that Lazarus be sent back to warn his five brothers who were still on earth. He did not want them to end up where he was. He was told that too was not possible. Abraham explained that if these brothers would not listen to the message God had delivered through Moses and the prophets, neither would it help if they heard from someone who came back from the dead.

Terrifying as these glimpses of Hell are in the Bible, what if they still fall short in describing what it will be like for those who choose to exclude God from their lives? Suppose the pastor was correct, and God finally does respect the wishes of those who want nothing to do with Him. From descriptions in Scripture, Hell will not be that desirable an experience! I do believe it's true that God can't have a relationship with us if we are not open to that relationship.

The Good in Life Remembered

Imagine someone says they are prepared to tell you something. Before they do, however, you are told that you must write it down. The impression you are given is that the message is especially important. In the last book of the Bible this type of instruction appears several times. We could probably agree that when something is written down it is certainly more permanent than if it is only spoken. A Chinese philosopher once said that, "The faintest ink is better than the strongest memory."

These messages in the Book of Revelation are sometimes communicated by a Voice from Heaven, sometimes by an Angel, and, in another instance, by The One seated on the Throne. I wish to single out one of these passages found in the 14th chapter of Revelation. It reads as follows: "And I heard a Voice from Heaven saying, write this, 'Blessed are the dead who from now on die in the Lord.' 'Yes,' says the Spirit, 'they will rest from their labors, and their deeds do follow them.'"

The word "blessed" means favored or fortunate. It can also mean--to be saved, redeemed, glorified--to be marked by God's favor. We might ask concerning this passage, who is it that is being called, "Blessed?" It is, "The dead who die in the Lord." From elsewhere in Scripture we know this means those who, in this life, have come to believe that Jesus is the Son of God. It is speaking here of persons of faith.

Death marks the end of a person's life. The assurance this passage gives is that when a person of faith dies, whatever good they have accomplished will not be forgotten. It will be preserved and remembered. And the results of the good they have done will follow them as they leave this present life and enter the next.

It is interesting that it does not say their works go ahead of them into Heaven. That might imply, that's how they were permitted to enter. Nor does it say their works squeezed in alongside them. That could signify their good works helped them gain entrance. No! It says, "...and their deeds do follow them." Whatever good they have accomplished in life will not be lost or forgotten.

Listen again to this message that was written down: "Blessed are the dead who from now on die in the Lord." "Yes," says the Spirit, "they will rest from their labors, and their deeds do follow them."

Swallow Up Death Forever

A friend of mine tells of an experience from his boyhood. He grew up on a farm in Minnesota. He and his family were members of a country congregation. The congregation was putting on a church supper and he and some other children were playing outside. Next to the church was a cemetery. My friend said, "There is no better place to play hide and seek than in a cemetery!" And that's what they were doing.

A woman of the congregation approached his mother and told her, "I don't think the children should be playing in the cemetery!" His mother had replied, "I know quite a few people buried out there, and I don't think they would mind a bit."

Because of God's plans in dealing with death, maybe God doesn't mind either. We read in 1 Cor. 15.26, "The last enemy to be destroyed is death." In very clear language we are told that God plans to get rid of death.

The Prophet Isaiah in an Old Testament passage (ch.25) proclaims the same message. In describing what will happen, we are told that the day will come when God will throw a great party. It will be a festival like no other! There will be plenty of the best food and well aged wines at this elaborate feast. And what is being celebrated is that God will have done away with death.

It says, "God will destroy… the shroud that is cast over all peoples, the sheet that is spread over all nations; he will swallow up death forever. Then the Lord God will wipe away the tears from all faces, and the disgrace of his people he will take away from all the earth, for the Lord has spoken.

"It will be said on that day, 'Lo, this is our God, we have waited for him, so that he might save us.'" In place of weeping and sorrow there will be laughter and a celebration. For God will have "swallowed up death forever."

Trust Future to God

Jesus had some things to say about the future. To a large crowd of people one day he said, "Do not worry about your life, what you will eat or what you will drink, or about your body, what you will wear. Is not life more than food, and the body more than clothing?

The future is like the horizon. It marks the limit of our vision. A friend of mine, a counselor, says we tend to worry about the future because we want to be "in control." Worry, he believes, is like a pointless prayer we pray to ourselves— a kind of idolatry where we seek to be the ones in charge.

However, the future is one thing the Lord has hidden from us. God sees the future, but as a loving parent he chooses not to burden us by letting us know what will happen in advance. Our attempts to control the future will therefore fail because it is beyond our reach.

Abraham Lincoln once told a story to illustrate this. When he was a young lawyer in Illinois, he used to ride the circuit with the judge from the county seat. One spring there had been a long spell of pouring rain, the brooks and creeks had been transformed into rivers. They were often stopped by these swollen streams and could cross them only with great difficulty.

But still ahead was the Fox River, much larger than all the rest. The judge and Lincoln kept saying to each other, "If the streams give us trouble, what will it be like when we get to the Fox River?" Darkness fell before they got there so they stopped at a tavern to spend the night.

After securing their night's lodging and something to eat, they were glad to see Peter Cartwright among the guests. As presiding elder he would have crossed the river in all kinds of weather. Certainly, he would know its ways. So, after the evening meal, they gathered around him and asked if he knew about crossing the Fox River. "Oh, yes," he replied. "I know all about the Fox River. I have crossed it often and know it well. But I have one fixed rule regarding the Fox River. I never cross it, till I reach it!"

Too often we attempt to cross our rivers before we reach them. We try to live a week in advance instead of one day at a time. "Which of you by worrying," Jesus said, "can add a single hour to your span of life?" Anxiety or worry won't lengthen life. It can only shorten it. Paul in one of his letters wrote: "Be anxious about nothing but tell God every detail of your needs in earnest and thankful prayer. And the peace of God which passes all understanding will keep your hearts and minds in Christ." The answer to our worry is a renewed reliance upon God.

Jesus Is the Way

It was the night before the crucifixion. Jesus had told his followers about his Father's House of Many Rooms. He was going there, he said, to prepare a place for them. But he would return to take them with him. Then he added, "And you know the way where I am going." Thomas, never afraid to raise questions or to express an opinion, said, "Lord, we do not know where you are going. How can we know the way?" Jesus said to him, "I am the Way…!"

It was something like that for a missionary who was on an island off the coast of New Guinea. The missionary needed to get from one end of the island to the other. Knowing he could not make the journey alone, he hired one of the natives as his guide. They started out early one morning.

The guide led the way through the jungle slashing the vines and heavy undergrowth with his machete. The missionary had counted on seeing signs of a path they would follow. He expected evidence that others had gone that way before. However, there were no such signs, only heavy undergrowth. The farther they went the more the missionary began to wonder if the guide knew what he was doing.

His doubts finally got the best of him. He stopped the guide and asked, "Are you sure this is the way?" At first the native didn't understand the question. When he finally did understand, he said in surprise, "Why, I am the way!"

As it was for the missionary, so it is for us. As followers of Jesus, we run the risk of beginning to doubt our Lord. Maybe that's why he began this sharing session by urging his disciples, "Believe in God, believe also in me."

If we strike off on our own or begin to lag, we run the risk of becoming hopelessly lost. Jesus was telling Thomas as he is telling us: If you want to get to your destination stick with me. I'll get you there. There is no other path than the one I make for you. Jesus clarified what he meant by adding, "No one come to the Father but by me."

Paralyzed Man Walks

The Gospel writer Luke tells how four young men brought a friend of theirs to Jesus. They carried him on a stretcher because he was paralyzed and unable to walk. Arriving at the house where Jesus was, they faced a problem. The crowd was so large they couldn't get in. But they were determined. The roofs of houses in that area were flat. They somehow got their friend up on the roof. How they kept him from rolling off the stretcher we'll never know.

When they finally had him up on the roof, these resourceful engineers began removing tiles to let him down. The commotion would have captured the attention of everyone present. They probably had advice from the people below: "A little bit more this way."

Finally, they were able to lower their friend to the floor in front of Jesus. When Jesus saw their faith he said, "Friend, your sins are forgiven you." Imagine what those fellows up on the roof must have thought! That was not exactly what they had in mind in bringing him!

Meanwhile, a controversy broke out among those in the crowded room below. Some scribes and Pharisees were angry. Jesus had said what they considered blasphemy. "Who can forgive sins but God alone?" they asked.

Since Jesus understood their objection, he confronted it with a question: "Why on earth do you think evil in your hearts?" He asked. "Which is easier to say, 'Your sins are forgiven,' or to say, 'Stand up and walk'? So that you may know that the Son of Man has authority on earth to forgive sins"—he said to the paralyzed man, "I say to you, stand up and take your bed and go home."

Luke describes how the man stood up at once, picked up the stretcher on which he had been lying, and went to his home glorifying God. The faith of the four friends who brought him had been rewarded. And those who witnessed the miracle of healing said to one another, "We have seen strange things today."

The Road of Service

A song describes two roads back to Scotland and two Scottish Soldiers who are longing to return. They are both in a foreign land, but the one who sings the song has been sentenced to die. He therefore expects to reach Scotland before his friend because it will be his spirit and not his body that makes the journey. "O ye'll tak the high road and I'll tak the low road and I'll be in Scotland afore ye."

Jesus also spoke of two roads. There was the high road that seemed to lead to greatness. It could be described as the road of self-interest—of promoting one's own concerns at the expense of others. In contrast, there was the low road that appeared to have no future. It involved the giving of oneself in serving others. But Jesus assured his followers that it was the low road that led to greatness.

Jesus, in preparing for his final journey to Jerusalem, knew what awaited him there. He also told his disciples what was to happen. He said, "The Son of Man will be handed over to the chief priests and scribes who will condemn him to death. They will then hand him over to the gentiles to be mocked and flogged and crucified. But on the third day he will be raised."

Hardly had he said this when two of his disciples made a request. They asked him to give them places of prominence. They requested that they be allowed to sit, one at his right and the other at his left in his kingdom. Jesus' reaction was one of surprise. He replied, "You don't know what you are asking!" He explained that they might indeed experience suffering with him, but to bestow places of honor was something only his heavenly Father could do. The other disciples were upset. If he had granted the request, only positions of lesser importance could have been theirs.

The disciples had again misunderstood, so Jesus gathered them around him and said: "You know that the rulers of the gentiles lord it over others. Those considered great are tyrants over them. But it must not be so among you. Whoever wishes to be great among you, must be your servant. And whoever wishes to be first among you must be slave of all. For I came, not to be served, but to serve and to give my life as a ransom for many."

Life offers us both a high road and a low road. There is the prestigious road that everyone thinks leads to greatness but doesn't. And then there is a low road, the path of humility and of service. That low road may appear to go nowhere at first, but eventually it is the one that leads to honor. Jesus makes very clear; it is the low road he wants us to take.

Master of Wind and Wave

Jesus was speaking to a group of people gathered along Lake Galilee. As the crowd continued to grow, he got into a boat and moved slightly offshore. When evening came, he dismissed the crowd and said to his disciples: "Let us go across the lake to the other side." Lake Galilee is a fair-sized body of water in northern Palestine. Mountains bordering it on the north and west are separated by a steep valley. The geography of the Lake makes it subject to sudden changes in weather. Often you don't see a storm coming until it is upon you.

That night, as the sky darkened and the wind became violent, waves threatened to swamp the boat. They were taking on water fast. Jesus, however, was asleep at the back of the boat. Remember, he was the one who had suggested the journey. They were on the Lake because of him. Now he doesn't seem to care what happens to any of them. The disciples finally woke him saying, "Teacher, don't you care that we are perishing?"

Remember Job from the Old Testament. Job lived a prosperous life until one day he began experiencing one disaster after another. His first loss was his possessions. Then all his children were killed in a storm. Finally, his health failed. Adding to his misfortune, Job was forced to respond to the easy explanations of his so-called "friends." In the climax of the book, God asks Job, "Where were you when I laid the foundations of the earth?"

Ellie Wiesel, a survivor of both Auschwitz and Buchenwald during the Second World War, felt Job let God off too easy. Job should have turned the question back upon God himself. He should have said, "That's beside the point! I don't know where I was. But where were you when I was suffering? One tragedy after another invaded my life. Why were you silent? Why didn't you do something?" Those are questions we find ourselves asking in the face of unwelcome events. It might be a doctor's diagnoses of cancer. Or, our home is destroyed in a storm. Possibly there is a divorce within the family. Trouble comes as out of nowhere.

I'm not sure what the disciples expected from Jesus when they woke him. Did they think he would help bail out the boat? Or maybe they expected a powerful prayer from him to save them. What happened took them by surprise. It says, "When he awoke, he rebuked the wind and said to the sea, 'Peace, be still!' And the wind ceased and there was a great calm." The disciples asked the obvious question. "Who then is this, that even the wind and the sea obey him?"

Whatever storms engulf our lives, let us remember that the Lord is still with us God is not just a spectator. God has chosen to immerse himself in the difficulties of our lives.

Nature of Temptation

How much water outside a boat will sink it? That was the question I often asked a group of young people. After thinking about it they would clarify the issue. It wasn't the water outside that could cause a boat to sink. It was the water inside! That's true also for temptation. We may know other kids are "doing drugs," but it is when we entertain the thought of taking them ourselves that our boat begins to leak. We may know other students are cheating on exams, but it is when we decide to cheat that we begin "taking on water."

There is a mistaken notion that temptations come only when we are with others. It's true in some instances, but maybe the strongest temptations come when we are alone. It was that way for Jesus. He was in the wilderness by himself. One gospel writer says, "There were only wild animals nearby." It is in those times alone that we settle the issue of what we will or will not do. It is in solitude, with no outside interference, that we make the most crucial decisions of life.

Temptations are also aimed at the foundations of life. If Satan can undermine our faith, then he has us exactly where he wants us. Jesus had just heard the voice of his Heavenly Father saying, "You are my Son, the Beloved…." With that assurance ringing in his ears he was led out into the wilderness. Notice the first thing the Devil says: "If you are the Son God…." Why didn't he say, "Since you are the Son of God," or, "because you are the Son of God…." Instead, "If you are the Son of God" why don't you do these things? The real temptation was to distrust who he was—to doubt his call—to question his relationship with his Heavenly Father.

If Satan can get us to doubt God's love, or the possibility of our being forgiven, or the certainty of our salvation, then the battle is virtually over. There is nothing so paralyzing as doubt. That has been his method from the beginning. Satan got Eve to doubt God's fairness. If the foundation of a building can be destroyed, then the entire building's destruction is inevitable.

In times of temptation we need to keep our eyes on the Lord. Jesus focused his gaze on God. That is where his attention was. A friend of mine from seminary days tells about a dog he once had. My friend would place left-over meat scraps in front of him and then make him sit at attention until he was given the word, "Eat." The dog's mouth would drool with saliva as he anticipated the succulent food. But as he waited for the command, my friend said, he kept his eyes on me rather than the meat. "Perhaps my dog knew if his eyes were on the meat, he could not withstand the temptation." In times of temptation for us our eyes need to be fixed on Christ.

On Being Found

For their vacation a family rented a cabin on a lakeshore in northern Minnesota. The father, mother and a four-year old little boy named Jimmy planned to spend a week there. They invited one of the grandmothers to join them.

One day when Jimmy was taking a nap, the mother and grandmother decided to go for a walk. There were many trails from which to choose in this heavily wooded area. After they left, Jimmy woke up and wanted to know where they were. His father said they would be back soon. But Jimmy was angry. Why hadn't they taken him along? He was going to go and find them!

There was a hook high on the screen door that Jimmy's father could have secured. He could easily have kept his son from leaving the cabin. But instead he decided to let him go. Jimmy stormed out, slamming the door behind him. He started down one of the paths he was sure his mother and grandmother had taken.

His father let Jimmy go, but chose instead to follow, keeping out of sight behind shrubs and trees. The little fellow plodded along, firmly convinced he was going in the right direction. Every once in awhile he would stop and look around, but then that look of determination returned, and he marched on for close to half a mile. By now he was no longer on any kind of path. He still hadn't found his mother and grandmother, and he didn't know where he was or how to find his way back. He suddenly realized he was lost!

Just as he was about to burst into tears, his father stepped out from behind a tree and came walking towards him. With arms outstretched, little Jimmy ran to meet him saying, "Oh Daddy, I'm so glad I found you!"

You hear people speak of having "found God." When they do, I believe it can be compared to the experience of little Jimmy in the story. God keeps his eye on us and is never very far away. In a time of crisis, we finally realize our predicament and reach out to him. An Old Testament prophet quotes God as saying, "You will seek me and you will find me, when you search for me with all your heart." Felix Mendelssohn in a tenor aria recounts this same promise. "'If with all your hearts ye truly seek me, ye shall every surely find me.' Thus saith our God."

Blood's Ability to Speak

Can blood talk? Is blood able to speak? The author of one of the New Testament books says that it can. "You have come to Jesus, the mediator of a New Covenant and to the sprinkled blood that speaks more graciously than the blood of Abel." Strange indeed! Human attributes assigned to blood itself!

In recent times we have learned that blood carries a genetic code. The blood of everyone is unique to that person. So, blood can identify the individual to whom it once belonged. Convictions in a court of law have been affirmed or overturned based on what samples of blood at a crime scene were able to tell.

This passage from Hebrews points back to what happened between two brothers. Cain became jealous of his brother Abel. He plotted to take his younger brother's life and then killed him. The Lord said to Cain, "What have you done? The voice of your brother's blood is crying to me from the ground!" The ground had received a stain that could not be removed. Innocent blood had been shed.

Centuries later under the leadership of Moses and at God's direction, a whole sacrificial system was set up for the Israelites. Blood from their offerings became the way they pleaded for God's forgiveness. The priest would take a basin of blood drawn from an animal sacrifice. He would then sprinkle this on the people. Another basin of blood was brought into the holiest place in the Temple and poured on the Ark of the Covenant which contained the Ten Commandments. God would hear the people's plea for pardon and forgive.

This was all a preview of a much more important sacrifice that God himself was prepared to make. God would make the one supreme sacrifice in offering up his Son. "For God so loved the world he gave his only begotten son that whoever believes in him may not perish but may have eternal life."

The blood of Abel was shed against his will. Jesus gave his life freely and willingly. Jesus said before his crucifixion. "I am the Good Shepherd. The Good Shepherd lays down his life for the sheep. No one takes it from me, but I lay it down of my own accord. I have power to lay it down, and I have power to take it again."

Some years ago, the teacher of a 3rd grade class asked her students what happened on the first Good Friday. One little boy was eager to answer. "That was the day," he said, "that Jesus died on the Red Cross." It's true, the cross was red! Red with the blood of Jesus. Because Jesus willingly gave up his life for our sins, God was able to promise eternal life through faith in him.

Importance of Give in Forgiveness

At the heart of the word "forgive" (or forgiveness) is the shorter word "give." When you "give" something to someone you must let go of it. You cannot hang onto whatever it is you are giving away. When it comes to forgiving someone, it is essential to "let go" of whatever wrong or injustice that has been done to you. If you hang onto the injustice, you have not really forgiven the other person. Nelson Mandela is quoted as saying that if he had not been willing to forgive those who imprisoned him for 27 years, he would still be in prison.

A new insight for me, that I believe is closely related to forgiving another person, is the matter of forgiving yourself. In any relationship you have, who is the person you see the least clearly? It is in fact yourself. That insight came as I was present when a husband and wife were in a heated argument. I knew this couple well. The person accusing the other of committing a wrong, I was aware, had committed the same wrong themselves. My hunch was that this previous wrong was something for which that individual had never sought or received forgiveness.

We understand the injustice done to us best when it is an injustice or wrong of which we also are guilty. That old concept is true, the one pointing a finger has three fingers pointing back at him or herself. Central to being able to forgive is coming to the place where we can forgive ourselves. A breakthrough can happen when we begin to see that forgiving someone must be done in tandem with forgiving ourselves. Quite often it is for a similar offence.

Picture a person with a dead carcass chained to their ankle. Wherever they go they must drag that old carcass with them. When we live with something we have been unwilling to forgive, we are like a person dragging dead meat behind. I call it a carcass because it is often something from long ago. Being able to forgive does involve giving something away.

I think this is what the Psalmist understood. "If you, O Lord, should mark iniquities, Lord, who could stand? But there is forgiveness with you that you may be feared." (Ps.130.3-4)

God sets the example of what it means to forgive. And central to the experience is "letting go!"

The Aroma of Christ

The Apostle Paul in his second letter to the people of Corinth refers to the message concerning Jesus as a lovely perfume that he and other Christians are privileged to wear (2.14-16).   Wherever we go, he says, "We are the aroma of Christ…." But then he makes the strange observation. To those being saved it is the refreshing fragrance of life itself. But to others it is the deathly smell of doom. To some, a perfume signifying life and to others at the same time the odor of death! How can that be?

As a young pastor I served a two-point parish. One congregation was in town and the other some twelve miles into the country. They represented two different communities with little in common except having the same pastor. Funerals often came in rapid succession with little time to prepare for a second or third one. So, I would often reuse a text and material from a sermon I had preached a short time before. Other than the introduction where I spoke of the deceased, the messages could be virtually the same. My effort at each funeral was to present the gospel as clearly and as helpfully as I could.

But on several occasions, I was taken by surprise. Let's say in one congregation the funeral was for a person who was a devout Christian with abundant evidence that they had been a person of faith. I sensed that those present found comfort and hope in my message. But a few days later, as I shared virtually the same sermon, the response was the exact opposite. Instead of comfort and hope, there was a reaction of fear and foreboding. If the person who had died had been a person of faith, they had kept it a secret even from those who knew them best.

The message concerning Jesus is like a lovely fragrance. It lets us know that God cares about us and has gone to great lengths to rescue us from sin and death. In John 3.16 we read, "For God so loved the world that he gave his only Son, that whoever believes in Him may not perish, but (instead) may have eternal life." It is what God has done for everyone, without exception. But it is still a gift!   And like all gifts, it can be accepted or declined. To those who have received it and therefore benefit from what God has promised, it is like a lovely perfume. To those who have rejected it, there is the deathly smell of doom.

Having Hope in God

When I went to bed last night, I didn't worry that morning would come. I was certain that it would—that a new day would dawn. So dependable is God's steadfast love, "that it never ceases," the Bible says. "His mercies never come to an end. They are new every morning."

The book of Lamentations in the Bible is not where you would expect to hear that message. Its five chapters describe one of the most painful periods in Israel's history. As a nation it had been conquered by Babylon. This book of the Old Testament is aptly named Lamentations because the word lament means "to mourn loudly—to cry out in anguish." Virtually the entire book is a lament.

But in the very center of the book there is a totally different message. It comes as a breath of fresh air, presenting a whole new perspective. You might say it gives the assurance that, "With God all things are possible!"

Hear once more those words from the 3rd chapter. "The steadfast love of the Lord never ceases. His mercies never come to an end. They are new every morning; great is your faithfulness. 'The Lord is my portion,' says my soul, 'therefore I will hope in him.' The Lord is good to those who wait for him, to the soul that seeks him. It is good that one should wait quietly for the salvation of the Lord." In other words, God's faithfulness is beyond our understanding. We should therefore place our hope in him.

The New Testament speaks of hope as an anchor of the soul. An anchor is dropped in the water from the bow of a ship. It serves its purpose as it falls to the bottom of the ocean and digs into something solid. A cable or chain attached to the anchor holds the ship in the safest position possible, facing into the wind.

When an anchor is being used you can't see it. It is out of sight. Its purpose is to prevent the ship from being driven with the wind. Interestingly enough, a New Testament book in the Bible has a similar pronouncement concerning hope. There we read, "Hope that is seen is not hope. For who hopes for what is seen? But if we hope for what we do not see, we wait for it with patience." The author then adds, "For in hope we were saved."

Gratitude Brings Joy

A pastor friend of ours lost his wife some time ago. His wife suffered a stroke resulting in her untimely death. In a letter my wife and I received a short time later, he shared a sentence he keeps on his refrigerator door. The sentence reads, "Gratitude changes the pain of loss into a peaceful joy."

It is a quotation from Dietrich Bonhoeffer, a German pastor who opposed Adolph Hitler. Bonhoeffer was imprisoned by the Nazis. Only a few days before the end of the 2nd World War he was executed on the express orders of Hitler.

While in prison, Bonhoeffer had written a series of letters that were smuggled out by the guards. In his letters he spoke of what it was like to lose his freedom and to live daily with the threat of losing his life. For Bonhoeffer and for our pastor friend, you would think there was nothing for which to be thankful. But the Bible says, "Seek, and you will find." In life we tend to find that for which we are looking. If we are searching for things about which to complain, there will be plenty of these. Many of us are at a time in life when loss is a familiar experience.

For some it is the loss of no longer being able to drive a car. For others it is the fact of being unable to live alone. It might have to do with losing our hearing, or problems with our sight. The greatest loss is the death of someone whom we love—a marriage partner, another family member, a close friend.

When our friend's wife died, he was soon to retire. The following summer they had been looking forward to a trip to Norway. When all this changed, should this pastor focus on the altered plans or on their many experiences over the years? They had raised a family of four gifted sons. They had been able to enjoy several grandchildren. Together theirs had been a rich ministry in several parishes. By posting this on his refrigerator door, our friend was reminding himself where he wanted his focus to be. There is a song that encourages us to do the same:

> "When upon life's billows you are tempest tossed,
> When you are discouraged, thinking all is lost,
> Count your many blessings; name them one by one,
> And it will surprise you what the Lord has done."

If any of us makes the effort to count our blessings, the list is long indeed. It helps us focus on a gracious God who provided them. Gratitude can change the pain of loss into a peaceful joy!

Facing Life's Disappointments

When our daughter was six years old, my sister in California sent a wedding dress she made for her. The following spring, I vividly remember the day our daughter ran across the street to show the dress to an older couple. They were like grandparents to all our children.

Half an hour later I was sitting in the shade of our driveway reading a book when she came running back, skirts flying in the wind. Before she climbed into my lap, I pictured what it would be like some day in the future to walk her down the aisle for a real wedding.

The day came about nineteen years later when a young medical school graduate proposed. Our daughter by then had graduated from college and was planning to go to law school. Those plans were changed with their approaching marriage. She got a secretarial job instead. First a son was born to them and then two daughters. They moved with their family to what she called, "her dream home."

Fourteen years into their marriage, her husband moved out of their home. A couple years later he filed for divorce and has since remarried. About a year later, our daughter moved with her three children to a smaller house she could afford. Early on, in talking to their teenage son, she asked how he felt about the separation. His two-word answer was, "It sucks!" She said, "That's exactly how I feel."

By taking some additional courses, she was able to secure a position as a grade school teacher. Our daughter has accepted the situation in which she finds herself better than her father has. A statement she made to us more than once probably expresses it best. "It is what it is." I marvel at how she has coped with all the challenges she has faced. To say the least, I am extremely proud of her and of the love she has poured into the lives of these three grandchildren.

I can't help but think it is her faith in Christ that has sustained and kept her. Our Lord has promised all those who believe in Him, "I will never leave you or forsake you."—Heb.13.5. (I never expected to publicly share this disappointment. It is with our daughter's permission that I do.)

God's Will vs Our Traditions

A group of Pharisees and scribes one day asked why the disciples disregarded the teachings of the elders. The disciples had failed to wash their hands before they ate. Jesus replied with a question of his own. "Why," he asked, "do you break one of God's commandments for the sake of your tradition?"

Jesus then quoted one of God's commands where we are told, "Honor your father and your mother." Jesus pointed out that they had replaced it by telling their parents, "Whatever support you might have had from me is Corban (that is, an offering given to God)." In other words, to them their tradition was more important than what God had directed them to do.

A little over a year ago, a football player named Colin Kaepernick took a knee during the singing of the national anthem. In doing so he was protesting situations where persons of color had been killed at the hands of police. He pointed to two recent instances.

This sparked a national debate. On the one hand Kaepernick was calling attention to what he saw as a violation of God's command, "Thou shalt not kill." Those on the other side of the argument said that Kaepernick was disrespecting an accepted tradition in our country of standing for the singing of the national anthem.

Is anyone haunted, as I was, by a video of something that happened only a couple years ago? A police officer shot a black man. The man, whose name was Walter Scott, had been stopped because of a broken taillight.

A witness reported that the policeman had used his taser on Mr. Scott. When he began running to get away, he was at least 15 or 20 feet distant. The policeman fired his gun eight times and finally felled Mr. Scott who later died. A bystander captured this on camera, and we saw on television the attempted escape, the shooting, and the subsequent activities of the police.

I have agonized, as I hope you have, about the silent protest that began with one man kneeling at a football game. Kneeling in the Christian tradition is usually a sign of obeisance—of reverence or of deference. In other religions this is true as well.

There is much for which we are grateful here in America. I do not think anyone, black or white, should disrespect policemen whose work is difficult to begin with as well as dangerous. I for one want always is to show respect for our flag and the country it represents. But I want even more to listen to any cry for justice that I understand is important to God.

Experiencing Loss

Over the years I have made many visits to shut ins. In doing so, I have witnessed first-hand the losses people have experienced. The loss for some has been to no longer drive a car. For others, it has meant illness for themselves or a member of their family. In my visits I have sought to understand and to empathize with them. Recently, a member who decided several years ago to care for his wife at home confided just how difficult it has been. He said he had always thought of himself as being quite spry. He now admitted his stamina is not what it once was.

An experience of loss recently struck home to me personally. Ten years ago, I chose to have radiation for recently discovered cancer. Thankfully, that threat of cancer was removed. But the side effects may now be causing some unintended consequences. More than one person has told me, "Radiation is a gift that keeps on giving!" I am glad the radiation took care of the cancer, but I must admit this new problem, if it was caused by the radiation, has resulted in a different kind of loss.

Have you ever stopped to consider that, from infancy to old age, loss is a part of life? Even the child, before it is born, is about to notice a dramatic change. In its mother's womb every need has been met. The temperature remained constant. Food was provided continually. Even the removal of waste occurred automatically. But then the day of birth arrives! Each of these provisions disappear in what is the first of many losses they will experience in life.

Or consider the teenager who is much older now. Several changes take place when a person graduates from High School. They have been accustomed to being with their friends and fellow classmates each day. Now the entire class scatters to the winds. Even if they have promised their closest friends they will keep in touch, it doesn't always happen. Then, at some point, living at home also changes, along with having meals provided and laundry done. We may not have thought of these experiences before as losses, but that's what they are.

In case of marriage, a former way of life comes to an end. And, if a child is born, there is a loss of freedom for the couple. However, it is during the later stages of life that losses seem to multiply. The one redeeming thing is what the Apostle Paul referred to when he wrote, "I regard everything as loss because of the surpassing value of knowing Christ Jesus my Lord."

Forgiving and Forgetting

The Lord spoke through the prophet Jeremiah about a New Covenant God would make with his people. The final part of the God's promise was: "…for I will forgive their iniquity and remember their sin no more." (Jer. 31.34)

This passage from the Bible reminds me of a story from one of the textbooks I once used in teaching confirmation students. The story involved a teenager named Mike and his younger brother Erik. One sweltering summer day Mike was changing oil on his car. He had just drained the dirty oil into a container and was putting the drain plug back into the oil pan.

The wrench he needed was lying over by the garage, so he asked Eric, his three-year-old brother, to get it. Eric went over and picked it up. But on the way back he had to pass the bucket of dirty oil. Eric looked at the oil in the bucket and couldn't resist. He dropped the wrench into the oil.

Mike, who was lying sweating under the car, heard it drop. Sliding out from under the car he saw what Eric had done and then blew up! "Eric, you stupid little brat," he yelled. "Can't you do anything right?" He picked Eric up and set him down firmly next to the garage wall. "You sit here, and don't you move until I tell you!"

Mike fished the wrench out of the oil and wiped it clean. As he knelt to slide back under the car, he heard a sniffle. He looked over at the garage where Eric was sitting. Eric had his hands folded and his eyes were big with tears. Mike went over and picked him up. "I'm sorry I yelled at you, Eric," he said. "I know you're sorry about the wrench. I forgive you for dropping it in the oil. Let's forget all about it!"

A minute later, Eric was bending down under the car. "Mike," he said with tears still in his eyes, "I'm sorry I dropped wrench." "What wrench was that?" Mike said. "I don't remember any wrench." Eric was quiet for a moment. Then a big smile spread across his face. A word of forgiveness had been spoken and received! It's that way when we confess our sins to God. He forgives and then is willing to forget. Incredible as it sounds, the Lord promises to have a short memory!"

Repentance a Change in Direction

Several years ago, I went with two carloads of teenagers from the parish I was serving to a camp in the Black Hills called Outlaw Ranch. For many of the youth who traveled with me to Outlaw Ranch that summer, the campfires and trail rides were a new experience.

However, what took place one evening around a campfire stands out in my memory. On a hill a quarter mile from camp was a cross. To get to that hill we had to cross a valley. One evening the entire group of campers and counselors gathered for a songfest beneath that cross.

Later that evening, all of us were given two small slips of paper. On the one, we were asked to write some sin for which we asked God's forgiveness. We were then invited to throw this piece of paper into the fire signifying God's promised pardon. On the other paper we were to write in code letters a request of something we asked God's help to overcome. This piece of paper we were to keep and take with us as a reminder. I have no way of knowing how this impacted others that night, but for me it become a change in direction.

On a road or highway, when you discover you are going the wrong way, it is time for a U-turn. This is properly called, "repentance." We may usually think of repentance as being sorry for something. However, the Bible speaks of repentance as "a directional word" rather than "an emotional one." Which way will I go?

Isn't that what Jonah needed to do? God said, "Go to Nineveh," and he went in the opposite direction. Jonah boarded a ship to Tarshish which is believed to be modern day Spain. He went the "wrong way!" It took three days in the belly of a sea monster for Jonah to finally "turn around" and do what God asked him to do.

In my prayers during recent months, one of my requests has been that God would help us as individuals and as a nation to repent. The word "repent" means to turn from that which displeases the Lord back to God. This might be a good time to evaluate and see if we are going the wrong way---as persons, as a family, as a congregation, as a nation. I wonder what impact it could have if this repentance were to take place!

Slow Down! Be Still!

Those who wrote the Psalms often spoke in behalf of the Lord himself. In one such instance the psalmist says: "Be still and know that I am God! I am exalted among the nations; I am exalted in the earth." (Ps.46.10)

A pastor serving a congregation out east told of his experience while traveling. He had made the trip to Honduras and back on three separate occasions. Instead of going by passenger ship he had traveled on a slow-moving freighter. He said he liked the informality of that kind of vessel. He could get to know the captain and the crew. They would allow him on the bridge to see firsthand how plans were made for the ship to keep its course.

He described how, on their most recent voyage, the return destination was Albany, NY. They were carrying 133,000 forty-pound boxes of banana. Coming north out of Baltimore the ship made its way through the Chesapeake and Delaware Canal. This waterway is about twelve miles long. Using the canal shortens the trip by at least eight hours.

As they glided through the narrow passageway, they came to a marina on the port side. On a sign, plainly visible for everyone to see, were seven words: "Slow! You are responsible for your wake." A wake is the track or trail left by a boat in the water.

The universal rule of the sea is that a ship is responsible for the wake it generates. At over 8,000 tons, with a draft of twenty-seven feet, a freighter going full speed through this tight body of water would play havoc with yachts anchored on shore. Small boats would quickly become driftwood. A ship, capable of doing eighteen knots at sea, needs to slow down to at least four or five knots as it makes its way up the Hudson.

There are times when we need to slow down as well—to become quiet in God's presence. It is the Lord who is "our refuge and strength, a very present help in trouble." There is no better time for us to slow down than in the weeks of summer. It is during this season we are summoned to "Come and behold the works of the Lord." So, in the words of that sign and of Scripture: "Slow down! Be still and know that God is God"

God of Surprises

In his book, "Giants in the Earth," Ole Rolvaag tells about a traveling preacher who stops one day at this settlement of Norwegian newcomers. Accustomed to taking charge, he gives orders for everyone to assemble for a communion service in the largest of the humble homes. The theme for his sermon that day is, "The Glory of the Lord." As he preaches this lengthy sermon, the gathered group is listless and inattentive. He struggles to continue even though he thinks his efforts that day are a complete failure.

Finally, in his conclusion, the minister launches into telling a story about a recently arrived immigrant. She is a widow with nine children. She has heard of the dangers faced by others in her situation, so she goes to great lengths to protect her precious offspring. She uncoils a long rope that she has tied around her waist. She attaches the rope to each of her children. As she parades through the streets of New York City, she becomes a laughingstock to all who see her. The minister goes on to apply this to God's concern for every one of them.

The minister is speaking to an assembly of recently arrived immigrants who know what it means to be laughed at. These formerly inattentive worshippers hang on every word. God speaks powerfully to them that day through a message and a sacrament they will remember for the rest of their lives.

The preacher who has delivered the sermon, on the other hand, is critical of his efforts. He blames himself for using such a mundane illustration. He thinks his sermon has been a total failure. He leaves the settlement having no idea how God has blessed his efforts.

I believe God is one who delights in bringing about the unexpected. God often works to accomplish his gracious will despite what we regard as failure. We may think we have been defeated, only to discover God's purposes have been accomplished despite us. We have a God of Surprises!

To Honor God's Name

When we address God using the words of the Lord's Prayer, the first request we make is that God's name will be honored. Jesus taught this prayer to his disciples and they passed it on to us. Many of us know the prayer by heart. "Hallowed be Thy Name," is how the prayer begins. Strange that our Lord would place that first! Maybe it's because, if we do not use God's name respectfully, any pretense of praying would be a mockery.

Did you ever try buttoning your shirt or blouse starting with a button in the wrong buttonhole? If the first button is in the wrong place, so are all the rest. The wrong use of God's name can have the same effect. We address the prayers we offer to the One above all others. God's Name certainly deserves to be used respectfully or not at all. Yet we hear God's Name spoken carelessly many times a day. Recently one of our grandchildren responded to something they heard on television by exclaiming, "Oh, my G…."

How would you like it if every time something went wrong in another person's life, they would speak your name as if you were the one responsible? I doubt you would appreciate the undeserved attention. Apparently, God doesn't like it either. But all too often God's Name is used carelessly, or to no purpose.

Garage mechanics in their work have a small clip that is shaped like a miniature hair pin. I understand they call it, "the Jesus pin." The reason they give it that name is that when one of them is dropped, the pin is virtually impossible to find. So, mechanics usually say: "Aw Jesus, there goes another one!" It's sad that when something is lost our Lord gets blamed.

I remember a trip I once took with a group of college students. Another single fellow and I shared the same room for sleeping accommodations. For this college student, using God's name as a swear word was so much a part of his conversation, he was totally unaware of doing it. One day, as diplomatically as I knew how, I called it to his attention. I remember his total surprise.

In the New Testament book of James, the author speaks about prayer. He says, "From the same mouth come blessing and cursing." The author then goes on to say, "My brothers and sisters, this ought not to be…!"

A Person's Worth

One of my seminary professors wrote human interest stories in the form of poems. These he later published. In one of his poems he described a little boy whose class was preparing a dramatic presentation of the story of Peter Rabbit. The boy talked about it nonstop to his family and friends. As the day drew near, excitement ran high both at home and at school.

But when the special day came there was a big disappointment. The boy was sick and couldn't attend. His mother was especially concerned. She worried that her son's part would be missed. But the little actor said, "Don't worry Mom, the teacher's got two whole rows of cabbages." In other words, no one would realize he wasn't even there!

This story prompts another. It is about something that happened in my last year at seminary. Along with several other students, I took part in a summer of clinical training. The course was held at one of the mental hospitals in Minnesota still in operation in the 1950's. We received hands on experience working with mentally ill patients at the hospital.

However, during that summer one of the patients died. She was a woman in her sixties with no known relatives. The hospital administrator asked if our class would have a funeral for her. She was to be buried in a small cemetery on the hospital grounds. One of the pastors from the group agreed to conduct a brief service. The rest of the class and a few staff members became the assembled congregation.

When the service was over, no one was in a hurry to leave. Everyone was fully aware that none of us really knew her. No relatives had visited or shown concern. When the funeral ended, there was an almost painful silence. It was broken by one of the students near the back of the group. He asked a question: "What was she worth?" The pastor's homily had informed us that the woman's few possessions fit easily in an old cigar box.

At first no one spoke. But then, another student chose to answer by saying, "She was worth God!" In the light of our Christian faith, God placed this value on everyone. God asked Jesus his Son, who was without sin, to die for every other human being. By raising Jesus again from the dead, God made possible salvation for all who would believe. It really is true that we are not just, "one of the cabbages."

Our Admission of Being Like Sheep

"The Lord is my shepherd..." That's how the 23rd Psalm begins. But if we speak the Psalm as David did, we are admitting that we are sheep! We may have thought the comparison was a positive one. However, the opposite is true. Sheep can accurately be described in three ways. They are dirty, dumb, and defenseless.

A nursery rhyme gives a favorite image of sheep. "Mary had a little lamb. Its fleece was white as snow...." But contrary to that description, the reality is that a sheep is one of the dirtiest animals there are. A sheep is even dirtier than a pig. A pig enjoys playing in the mud, but its bristles are short and not much dirt will cling to it. A sheep on the other hand is like a walking dust mop. It collects every twig or burr, every bit of dust with which it comes in contact.

In the country of Palestine there is a custom, I have been told. At the end of each day, the shepherd kneels and rests his long staff on his shoulder. He then calls each sheep by name. They pass under the staff, and as they come close to the shepherd, he removes any thorn or thistle in their wool. When he finds a cut or bruise, the shepherd pours oil on the wound to help it heal. If we recite this psalm, "The Lord is my shepherd," it becomes an admission of being dirty. And as sheep we need at the end of every day the help and attention of our shepherd.

A second characteristic of sheep is that they are dumb. Cattle, by contrast, can be turned loose on a range to fend for themselves. They seem to have the instinct to find both water and good grazing. Not so the sheep. There could be an abundant water supply and lush pasture over the next hill, but they go in the opposite direction. For that reason, they need the shepherd as their guide. We are much like sheep in this way too. God's word is readily at hand, but all too often we choose the recreational or entertainment event instead.

A third attribute of sheep is that they are virtually defenseless. A sheep may be of comparable size to a dog, but a dog has strong jaws. Once they clamp those jaws on their enemy they are not about to let go. A cat has sharp claws. When danger threatens, they can usually claw their way out of any trouble. A horse has powerful hooves with which to kick its enemy. Or, it can turn tail and run. Not so the sheep. The sheep needs a shepherd to protect it. The rod that is mentioned in the Psalm is the club like weapon the shepherd carries to drive off whatever threatens his sheep.

In reciting this Psalm, we make the same claim that David did. The Lord is our Shepherd. But it also becomes an admission that we share the characteristics of sheep. We admit to being dirty, dumb, and defenseless.

Jesus' Invitation to Come

It happened in a mission school in Arizona. A teacher had shared with her students the passage from Scripture where Jesus invites persons who are troubled to come to him. He promises to those who do, that he will give them rest. Our Lord goes on to say, "For my yoke is easy, and my burden is light."

The teacher explained that a yoke was a piece of wood laid across the necks of two animals. The yoke joined them together for a common purpose. She then asked the children: "What do you think Jesus' yoke is?"

The children appeared puzzled by the question. They looked at their teacher and then at each other. The students shrugged their shoulders. After a pause of several minutes, a little girl at the back of the class timidly raised her hand. When the teacher called on her, she said, "I think Jesus' yoke must be when he puts his arm around your shoulder."

Listen again to this passage from Matthew's Gospel. Jesus said, "Come to me, all you who labor and are heavy laden and I will give you rest. Take my yoke upon you and learn of me, for I am gentle and lowly in heart, and you will find rest for your souls. For my yoke is easy and my burden is light."

I marvel at this child's insight as well as her explanation. I like that picture of Jesus and His arm around my/your shoulder when we respond to his invitation to come.

Oldest Christian Hymn

Irish tune—Londonderry Air
Arrangement by—Pastor Kermit Rye

Christ Jesus who, though in the Form of God, did not demand his rights as the Divine,

But laid aside his mighty power and glory, and took the form of a slave, becoming man.

And yet as man he was humbled even more, becoming obedient even unto death,

And in his death, he died as a criminal, giving up his life upon that cruel Roman cross.

Therefore, God honored Him above all others, giving him a Name above all other names,

That at his Name every knee should bow, upon this earth, below and above as well,

And every tongue confess Him as the Lord, that God His Father might be glorified,

Therefore rejoice, and again I say rejoice, that all may know that the Lord is near at hand.

That all may know that the Lord is near at hand.

These words are from the New Testament. They appear in the second chapter of Paul's Letter to the Philippians. They are part of a text that reads like poetry. It is written in meters, systematically arranged. Many scholars believe it is an early Christian hymn Paul borrowed and incorporated in his letter. Maybe it was because it said so beautifully what he wanted to say. Paul introduces the hymn with the words: "Let the same mind be in you that was in Christ Jesus:" Then following are the words of the song. To complete the second stanza of the hymn, I have drawn on a couple verses from the fourth chapter of the same letter. If it was indeed a hymn, it may have been known by the congregation to which Paul writes. The tune that once accompanied it would, of course, long since have been forgotten This may well be the oldest Christian hymn we have.

Come, Thou Fount of Every Blessing

Come thou Fount of ev'ry blessing, tune my heart to sing thy grace;

Stream of mercy, never ceasing, call for songs of loudest praise.

While the hope of endless glory fills my heart with joy and love,

Teach me ever to adore thee; may I still thy goodness prove.

Here I raise my Ebenezer: "Hither by thy help I've come";

And I hope, by thy good pleasure, safely to arrive at home.

Jesus sought me when a stranger, wand'ring from the fold of God;

He, to rescue me from danger, interposed his precious blood.

Oh, to grace how great a debtor daily I'm constrained to be;

Let that grace now like a fetter bind my wand'ring heart to thee.

Prone to wander, Lord, I feel it; prone to leave the God I love.

Here's my heart, oh, take and seal it; seal it for thy courts above.

Text: Robert Robinson, 1735-1790

About the Author

Kermit J. Rye grew up on a farm in southeast South Dakota. He graduated from Augustana College in Sioux Falls and Luther Seminary in St. Paul, MN. For three years he served a three-congregation parish in Wittenberg, WI. He then traveled to Scotland where he took additional theological courses at the University of Edinburgh New College.

Upon returning to the States he served a parish at Elk Point, SD for nine years. He then served congregations in Iowa—fifteen years at Grundy Center and nine years at Estherville. He and his wife Doris have two sons, one daughter and five grandchildren.

www.ingramcontent.com/pod-product-compliance
Lightning Source LLC
Chambersburg PA
CBHW080919160726
48000CB00009B/3056